What's Not to Love?

Poems by Janet Beardsall
Illustrations by Devon Artists

First published in 2014 by
Janet Beardsall
Orchard House, Lower Broad Oak Road, West Hill
Ottery St Mary, Devon, EX11 1XH

Printed by John Gaffney Design and Print
The Old Town Hall, The Flexton
Ottery St Mary, Devon, EX11 1DJ

ISBN 978-0-9550796-2-7

Dedication

This book is dedicated to my friends Averil, Chris, Gill, Gloria, Hazel, Jean, Maggie, Pam and their families and to all who are suffering, or have suffered, illness and loss.

Contents

Thanks

Special thanks are due to Mary King MBE for very kindly taking the trouble to read my poems and for her generous remarks.

Many thanks also to Averil Gilkes and to the members of Trudy Longmire's Art Group who have kindly contributed illustrations.

Artist	*Illustration on Page*
Mary Atkinson	Dedication page
Averil Gilkes	Opp. page1, and 12, 15, 21, 26, 44, 48, 51
Dawn Offer-Hoare	3
Brenda Burville	4, 56, 59
Mary Stevens	5
Sue Dorey	7
Janet Beardsall	18
Dick Beardsall	25, 57
Mary Pike	35
Terrie Charles	45
Eileen Hawk	61

I would also like to thank my husband Dick for all his help in producing this book.

Hospiscare

Caring in Devon

Hospiscare is a local charity providing end of life care to patients and their families living in Exeter, Mid and East Devon. We have a 12 bed in-patient unit in Exeter as well as Day Care centres in Exeter, Tiverton and Seaton. Much of our work is carried out in the community with 26 specialist nurses caring for patients and families in their own homes.

We have recently launched an appeal to raise £250k to complete, equip, and run a new Day Hospice in Honiton for our patients and their families living in East Devon.

Our new Day Hospice will offer complementary therapies to patients, families and carers, an assisted bathroom for those no longer able to bathe at home, nutritious meals cooked by our catering team on site and a beautiful garden for a moment of peace. Time spent by our patients in the day hospice will give their carers some time to relax.

As a local charity we very much rely on the generosity and support of local people and businesses to raise the £4.1M that we need each year to continue providing our services. If you would like to know how you can help Hospiscare realise its vision to bring care closer to the people of East Devon please call Sarah Smith on 01392 688095, or email s.smith@hospiscare.co.uk.

The Hunter

When she goes out at night she
Always looks for him among the crowds.
Sometimes she doesn't see him
But when he appears
Head and broad shoulders above the rest
She feels that frisson only he can bring.

He's a giant among pigmies
More skilful than any of them
Always armed ready for action.
Light years ahead he
Outshines everyone around and is
Scintillating company.

She loves his silvery smile across the night,
His two dogs at his heels and
All the tales she's heard about him.
He's the centre of her universe.
She can't get enough of him
And could gaze at him for hours.

She'll miss him come summer.

Harry Mows the Lawn

Up and down the lawn he trudges,
Making long green straight smart stripes.
Stops sometimes to take a breather,
Sweating brow with kerchief wipes.

Such hard work for such an old man,
But it brings him quiet rewards -
Loves to smell the new-mown fragrance
And see straight stripes neat and broad.

Ah! that smell! – There's nothing on Earth
Fresher than that tangy scent.
Just one whiff, he's taken once more
Back to when, with eyes intent

And with hands clasped, he'd be waiting
Like a lion crouched down to spring,
Pounce upon the ball so swiftly,
Dive like swallows on the wing.

Playing cricket-how he loved it
When he was a little chap;
When the sun was always beaming
In those days of no mishap.

Punctually each Saturday he'd
Cycle through the heat-crazed noon,
Speeding past the nodding dog rose
In the hot dog days of June.

Afterwards, the mothers made them
Sandwiches and hot strong tea.
Sometimes they'd serve strawberries
And cream – a thrilling luxury.

And the laughter! – And the chatter!
And the tricks played on some boys!
Wipes away a tear as he sees
Long-dead days filled with such joys.

Yes – all gone, but he remembers
Each one clear as yesterday.
Spring-green days across the heat haze,
Shimmering, they fade away.

In the Cotswolds

Fight-the-ban posters nailed onto tree trunks
Red and green clashing high overhead.

Short narrow lane perched along upland
Ten times we stop to let lorries pass.

Six hundred years seen in the buildings
Of tiny toy towns veneered by today.

Fin-de-siècle feeling here from the cottage
In poplars, in hedgerows, in tall spanning skies.

Early on Sunday a tractor is vying
With birdsong, with voices and feeble church bells.

Decay in the orchard, along with the fruit farm
Abandoned in autumn, fruits rot where they fall.

Betty

For Fred and Jon

He did not go gentle. Nor did she: for
She loved husband, son, family and friends;
The freedom of the open road, bringing
New adventure; the complexities of
Cricket on a summer's day, cool in green
Shade beneath a whispering tree; a good read
By a cosy fire in winter; the long
White heat of baking beaches under turquoise skies;
And singing round a camp fire in the sapphire night.

She loved our greatest gift of all: her life;
And used that gift to give us memories
To cherish and hold closely in our hearts.
This was her biggest present to us here:
Our store of happy thoughts for future help, to turn
To anywhere, day or night; and there forever.

Paul

For Gloria and Derek

Peering over we can see his sunlit playground
stretching far and wide,
Suspended between two distant grey and rocky arms.
Here he would float and dream of swimming with
dolphins
In a warm, far-off sapphire sea, feeling calmed, lulled,
By the vast blue summer hammock cradling him,
As it rocked over the edge of the horizon and swung
back over the sands,
Tide on tide, wave on wave.

With a quick fish-flip forward he would
Dive down deep to
Hunt for shells, seaweed, crabs,
Pursue sand ripples and streaks of wavering sunlight,
Burst the surface like a seal then
Strike out, fast and strong in his blue, belovéd element.

Eye-level gulls cry above the sea's voice as it surges
onto rocks,
Gurgles in sump holes and tumbles along the shore,
far, far below us.

Out there he'd slice across the blue-fire sky,
Skim over the streaming breath of the sea as it
Roared and battled beneath him.
Wind-driven he'd race across its
Writhing back, sailing as free as air towards the shore
That he'd hardly begun to know.

Now silver moonlight fans out across the sleeping bay
Split by a gliding speck for a ghostly moment,
Then is shrouded by clouds
And passes.

Then

For ages I knew that I loved you
then
I thought I knew I loved you
(for ages)
then
I imagined I knew I loved you

(for ages I imagined and)
then
I knew I thought I loved you
then
I thought I thought I loved you
(for ages I imagined and
thought and)
then
I imagined I thought I loved you

then
I imagined I imagined I loved you
(then I)
then
I thought I imagined I loved you
then
I knew I imagined I loved you
(– knew).

On a Windy Night

On a windy night I saw you laughing in the stars
And felt your presence wrap around the sky.
You smiled across the stormy night
And outshone the moon.

Along the ribbon of the Milky Way you wandered
A great and wild-haired spirit striding near.
I saw your silent face glow down,
A soft and lovely light.

You shone like stars and moonbeams; an enigmatic ghost
Meandering freely in the starry skies.
When you and I are gone from earth
Our love will live in stars.

Someone unknown will someday look up at the sky
And catch a corner of our love as it darts,
Like a shooting star, across
The inky night of time.

Our tiny spark glimmering free in darkest space will last
To live for beings we will never see;
To live forever in star-filled nights
For searching unborn eyes.

It's Like This, Doctor

At nine o'clock I enter
My little surgery.
There're always crowds of folk who wait
For all their sakes I'm never late
They all depend on me.

I sit and listen to them
From nine o'clock till six.
They bring me problems, but no smiles:
There's Mrs Braithwaite with her piles
And Tom who needs his fix.

I sit and listen quietly
To all they have to say.
I hear it all with sympathy
And answer questions asked of me
Throughout the long, long day.

To them I'm not a person
I'm just a pair of ears.
They don't suppose I have my ills:
A wife who runs up great long bills
And has done so for years.

My eldest son is wayward,
My youngest one won't work.
My daughter sniffs coke when she can
She's sleeping with a married man –
An idiotic twerp.

My mother's in a wheelchair.
My father is insane.
My wife's unfaithful all the time –
Unfaithful with a friend of mine.
Thinks I don't know their game.

And I am being blackmailed
For some small past mistake.
I'm mortgaged right up to the hilt
I'm drinking whisky at full tilt
I'm secretly a rake.

But don't you worry, patient,
Your problem's mine, my work.
And don't you fret now, I'll stay dumb
Just sit here nodding, keeping mum
No duty will I shirk.

How close I hold your secrets
But closer still, hold mine.
For I've no one to hear me out
No one to turn to, cry, or shout
Or say, you're doing fine.

My problems are my burden
No one hears what I say.
In front of you a lonely man
Who's trying to do all he can
To keep the tears at bay.

John's Journey

On and on past fields of houses
TV masts on either hand
Peering through the smut-blacked windows
Into sprawling Metroland.

Snug inside the six-ten I sit
Roaring through the rushing night
Well-known rhythm how I love it
Don't I clutch my MS tight.

Hark! The church bells' tongues are ringing
Drifts of phrases floating free.
Hurry now, the kettle's singing,
Nanny's waiting up for me.

On Hearing the First Reading in Spring
(with apologies to Phil Spector et al)

I heard him read on Monday and my heart stood still
Da doo ron ron ron da doo ron ron
Standing so close, it gave me such a thrill
Da doo ron ron ron da doo ron ron
Yeah, my heart stood still
Yeah, his looks could kill
And when he read his poem
Da doo ron ron ron da doo - ooh ooh!

He caught us with his magic: one collective sigh
Da doo ron ron ron da doo ron ron
He spoke so quietly but my oh my
Da doo ron ron ron da doo ron ron
Yeah, didn't have to try
Yeah, I thought I'd die
And want him for my own
Da doo ron ron ron da doo – whoo hoo!

Got him on my mind now whatever I do
Da doo ron ron ron da doo ron ron
Men like him, so good, are very few
Da doo ron ron ron da doo ron ron
Yeah, hero worship you
Yeah, I love you too
And can I take you home?
Da doo ron ron ron da doo - boo hoo!

Even If He Had a Thousand Nets

Dark – so dark.
The friendly face of darkness wraps round like a velvet cloak
Rubs its purring face against his jaw and hands.

From the depths of this healing pool
Her face surfaces like a water lily.
Opens.
Shines like a star reflected on the night face of a pond.

Dark – so dark.
He holds her image in his mind's eye, willing it to stay,
Not become unseeable as the sun rises to burn
All stars from rivers, ponds, seas
And minds.

Only here true contemplation lies with him.
Night by night he gazes into eyes that can
Kill by vast waves of power.
Night by night he drowns deeper, deeper in dark pools
Full of silent stars.

Dark – so dark.
He holds her unblinking look in his mind's eye,
Draws comfort from deep midnight eyes that
Blaze intense like star-filled pools.
He holds her look, then drowns again
In fathomless depths of diamonds.

Night by night her star – filled eyes and mouth never
Answer, but glitter remotely in the dark.
Inaudible. Untouchable. Diamond hard. Sapphire silent.
She's ever present but unseeable until it's dark when

She reappears: a silent water lily
In the remotest depths of the velvet pool,
Unreachable always.
And like a cold star shining on the night face of a pond
She is uncatchable, forever.

Ethel Enjoys a Good Film

I like it when the strings begin to quiver,
That warbling trill gives me quite a shiver.
She sighs contentedly.

I like it when, against the background drone,
The hero claims her for his own dear own.
She swallows hard.

I like it when she falls into his arms,
And he protects her from the villain's harms.
She bites her lip.

I like it when the good guy has to go,
Rides in the sunset calling, "Goodbye Flo".
She blows her nose.

I like it when the people go all blurred,
And action's stopped, although the words are heard.
She wipes her eyes.

I like my weekly visit – it's so nice,
With box of chocs and hankies, chocolate ice.
She loves a good cry.

Our Mr. Entwhistle

"Now, where did I put your form?
Is it under here?
Maybe on the window sill –
Can you see it, dear?

May I trouble you to rlse?
No, not under there.
Maybe lodged behind the clock?
Underneath this chair?

In this drawer? – I'll take a peek –
Wrong again, my dear.
Ah! I have it! – In the desk! –
Empty there I fear.

Now if I could lay my hands –
Dear, dear – then I could –
Tell you all about the job,
Miss Tree – sorry, Wood.

Here at Banks' – your form, my dear! –
Well, I am surprised! –
We're very hot on strict routine.
We're highly organized!"

Too

Too much
Too soon
Now it's
Too late
To stop –
Too right.

Throwaway Times

Throwaway teabags
Throwaway food
Throwaway throwaway jars.
Throwaway papers
Throwaway tights
Throwaway throwaway cars.

Throwaway meaning
Throwaway words
Throwaway throwaway breath.
Throwaway learning
Throwaway jobs
Throwaway throwaway deaths.

Throwaway people
Throwaway sex
Throwaway throwaway lines.
Throwaway living
Throwaway love
Throwaway throwaway times.

Aunt Edna's Night Out

I like to go to my classes:
On Wednesdays I always troop
Along to the village hall,
To sit with folk in a group.

Our teacher's ever so pretty,
And ever so clever, too;
Although some of the things she says
Make the air turn somewhat blue.

I sit next to old Mr. Browning
And though he's so quiet and polite,
I've had lots of trouble with him -
At his age it doesn't seem right.

And Tom's just the same - you should see him,
Those evil looks that he gives.
Still, I can't really wonder at it -
Look at the way he lives.

Old Harry keeps having a snifter,
When we're s'posed to be having tea.
I can't understand what he says,
He mumbles so shockingly.

Mrs Braithwaite's so hard of hearing
You have to say everything twice.
Young Bobby just won't hold his tongue,
Interrupts, saying things that aren't nice.

I like to go to my classes,
They give me a well-earned break.
I've learned quite a lot from my little group:
They're a class of their own, no mistake!

Bathsheba

Sleek ginger cat.
Questing amber eyes that ask me whys
As you neatly curl in your cosy chair
And sigh contented sighs.

Stare ginger cat
As you sphinx-like sit, feet closely knit;
Washing your fur while you happily purr.
Safe in your basket sit.

Sleep ginger cat
As you lay on my back, loose and slack
Buzzing love-words, drowsy tunes in my ear.
 - Gone. Never to come back.

Lovely to See You

"That was Myrtle – you remember?
They'll be here by half-past eight."
"What! You don't mean Len and Myrtle?
And the house in such a state!"

"They were such an awful couple.
Always drunk – those tales he told!"
"She was always so tight-fisted
In her flashy clothes so bold."

Then they scurried, working quickly,
Dusting this and neatening that;
Straightening pictures, stuffing papers
Snug and safe beneath the cat;

Checking bottles, giving glasses
Each a final gleaming wipe.
"There's the door-bell" – "Oh! That Lego!"
– Hides it with a darting swipe.

"They're so early – Now, remember,
Please don't mention her crossed eyes.
– Oh, hello dears! Glad to see you –
Such a lovely, big surprise!"

Spiritual Cynthia

"Oh, Celia darling, what a pud!
I always love crême brulée.
Don't you, Sebastian, darling?"
"Yes dear, just as you say."

"Now tell me, how do you survive
Without a super micro?
I've bought a sweet little mixer –
Easy to work, you know.

Tell me the recipe, Celia.
Oh yes – so simple to do.
We're off to China on Monday –
Again – and what about you?

I always thInk it's too hot there
In August, you know, my dear.
Oh, Astrid's taking the children to
Venice, again, this year.

Well, Angie has a new pony,
And David his second T.V.
And Ted another computer –
Well, dear, it is only three.

And did you hear about The Car:
Our super-duper Jensen?
My dear, it's heavenly – lovely – far
Better than the Benson's.

I bought a dozen Hartnells for
I'd simply nothing, my dear.
They cost dear Seb a small fortune –
But should do for this year.

Oh! Seb, dear – we simply must fly!
We're sorry to leave so soon.
Must have an early night, tonight –
It's church for us at noon!"

Broken

In a blink of an eye their friendship died.
Trees bowed their heads
Birds wailed
The sun hid.

Winter swooped down
To wither all women to crones with a kiss,
To freeze all delight to death overnight
And to peck out his love in a heartbeat.

Hill Forts

Great Eggardon and Hambledon,
Pilsdon Pen and Maiden too,
How I love you, how I miss you.
How I long to be with you.

Hill forts of those ancient dead men,
Pagan fathers of our race,
I would love to see again your
Green and multi-wrinkled face.

It's so thrilling to stand bird-high,
Looking over views below;
See the fields like patchwork spreading
Miles away, then seaward go.

Feel the wind touch gently, softly,
Brushing past my sky-turned face;
Puffing grasses, flowers down-bent
Nodding, as I rejoin space.

Great clouds massing, melting, changing,
Covering the blazing sun;
Over fields huge shadows gliding,
Mirroring their onward run.

And the silence is uncanny –
As if someone's next to me –
Reach out, touch it; all enclosing,
Wrapping with its arms of green.

From below strange voices drift up,
Floating from the valley low.
Sheep bells ringing, cut the silence
With each tiny tinkling blow.

Over there a hawk is hovering
Silently above his prey.
On the sheep-trail sheep are treading
Indian-file along their way.

See the fox that runs so quickly,
Stealthily, across the hill.
Stops, with ears pricked, looking round him,
While he stands so quiet and still.

Dead homes of those long-dead pagans,
Older than our history.
Favourite places which seem homely,
Places which feel right to me.

As the red sun slowly slips down,
Hides behind the darkening hills,
Shadows creep out from the hollows;
Men seem to be living still.

Stealthy shadows all surrounding,
Shadows, long, of ancient men;
Feel their presence here beside me,
Feel their welcome home again.

And their presence is uncanny –
As if someone's next to me –
Someone I can almost touch; feel
Almost, but never see.

I belong here with these spirits.
I belong here with these roots.
Here our life began its journey;
Here the taproot of the shoots.

Hands across the ages reach out,
Gently pulling, tugging me;
Draw me to my origins: Great
Hill Forts – that I long to see.

Household God

"I don't know where we go to, no
Dear, after we are dead.
It's half past ten, so get up quick –
I've got to change your bed.

I don't know why we have the bomb.
Now come on, off you go.
I've got this room to spring-clean
Time's getting on you know.

I don't know if there're fairies, luv,
Or angels in the sky.
Now can you move your books and things –
I've got to make a pie.

I don't know if there is a God –
I'm only your mum, right?
You'll have to wait and ask your Dad
When he comes home tonight."

Join the Big Switch Off

"Be a doer
Not a viewer.
Switch it off. Stretch out your hand.
Switches are for
Turning off. You're
Living in cloud-cuckoo land.

Don't be lazy.
It's so easy
Flick off all those fantasies.
By a tiny
Knob so shiny
Click into reality.

Silver screen is
Rushing always:
Cardboard cut-out images.
Seeing one view,
Second-hand, you
Soak it up like soft sponges.

Join the living
Pleasure giving.
Take part in the world that's now.
Life evading….."
"Picture's fading.
Rotten programme, anyhow."

Out of Reach

The Ming vase in the window was what he wanted,
But it was too expensive for him to buy, to hold, to look
at almost.
Ring-fenced it stood alone, too rare and precious to
possess.

Beyond the pale he stood, excluded and poor,
Hardly daring to glance, too dumbstruck to ask.
Do Not Touch, a notice said, behind the sheet of glass.

Even knowing that some things cannot be had, ever,
He itched to make a smash-and-grab and run for it, but
couldn't:
Spellbound, rooted, he could only peer through a
miasma of longing.

Now he stands at the edge of a brittle sea
Staring at a watery-green desert
Mending his heart daily over and over.

But like the tide the longing returns
And he drowns again as she slips from his grasp
And he shatters like a teacup.

Weeding Out

In the dusky green steep-sided evening
He gardened in the gathering pools of night
That rose up cool and rippling round his feet.
He waded in the ebbing warmth of day
With birdsong showering down from every tree.

Knee-high nettles choked untended flowerbeds
And bindweed strangled everything it touched.
Low-flying bats, displaying, darted and criss-crossed.

Sweating in the hell of evening he hacked
And sliced with all his strength, working fast to
Clear the ground before night fell to stop him.

As angry as an unpaid landlord he hauled
A squatter mini-oak out of its bed.
Ruthlessly he banished the uprooted plant:
In seconds years of tender growth were dead.

Eleven now. He opens wide the door onto a dark world
Lit by half a moon, silent but for the whirring of
moths' wings
And fat toads rustling in dank flowerbeds.
At last he revels in the peace: today
He evicted her forever from his heart.

Simon's Soliloquy

I'd like to be a pop star –
Be rich and famous, like.
I would shake me 'ips,
And I'd stretch me lips,
Like Mick Jagger does, over 'is mike.

I'd shut me eyes up, tightly,
And then, throw back me 'ead.
To the girls' delight
Through me teeth, clenched tight,
I would mutter words, never yet said.

I'd have me 'air done fancy:
Some 'anging down me face;
Then 'ave two bald stripes
Near me ear 'oles, like;
An 'ave ribbons – all over the place.

Now – what about me makeup?
Well, green lips for a start;
And a silver patch,
Over one eye, natch;
And me nails painted red, like a tart's.

Me clothes? – Well, let me see now –
A singlet, full of 'oles;
And me trousers, tied,
With string, six-inch wide;
And a red satin jacket – years old.

And when I'm rich and famous
The biggest star for years
I'll buy Dad a car –
"Yes, luv – here you are.
Eat up! You'll be late for school, dear!"

Miranda's Painting

There are apple trees in the moonlight
Grey clouds of blossom floating
In blue-green seas of leaves.
The grass is a dark green sky
Lit by gold flower-stars
And the moon-gazing girl dreams
Lost in thought on her swing.
The little lost girl.

We've moved it from room to room.
It's hard to place here
Our colours are light, pale,
More daytime than dark.
It's summertime too
And so it's difficult –
You know, it's not really that.
It's her. She feels so lost.

Each time we see it
We think of our holiday
Which seems like a dream.
Another world: green and lost,
Tree-filled and tranquil.
A place where you could
Drift in a green dream
Lost in thought, like her.

Who is the girl in the moonlight
Who haunts our house now
In her ghostly world that
Won't mesh with ours?
Our peaceful dreams have vanished
And our hopes of an orchard are moonshine.
The world is full of darkness
And twilit sad lost girls.

Off Stage

Malcolm is waiting in the wings.
He's practised his stance
And his breathing.
Now he's getting into the part.
He tosses his long auburn curls
And rolls his eye over the set,
Thinking over his lines.
He's looked at his messages:
Andy and Trevor are on tour;
Gilly's in rep this summer
And Jonathon's on telly.
So depressing, darling.
What will he do at the end of October?
This lot will close
Then he'll be back on the dole,
Scanning the ads, visiting agents all winter.
Too awful to think of, luvvie.
Well. Here come the punters.
He takes a deep breath and projects:
"Will it be tea or coffee, Madam?"

Fish Out of Water

She glided along the seafront
In a coat of fur scales,
Sleek silver head shining
Turning this way and that,
Blue eyes never blinked.
Open-mouthed, she gazed at the water,
Sky and buildings along the margin,
Progressing purposefully, smoothly,
Without a ripple, towards her prey.

She met him for lunch:
Pounced and gobbled him up, easily,
With a snap of her powerful jaws; then
Swished contemptuously out of the restaurant,
Dived towards the car park,
Slithered like an eel into
Her shark of a car
And with a flick of her tail fin,
Darted away.

The Beacons at Firle

Sussex was blue and green.
France, red, yellow and orange.
Italy, terracotta and purple.
Every year coloured in.
Distances scrutinised.
Light assessed.

Hold my hand, she whispered,
As they lay, side by side, in the dark.

Houses full of flowers,
Pictures, wall paintings.
A hotchpotch of furniture
And continental crockery.
Tables, chairs, beds, doors:
Every surface, decorated.

Reluctantly, he held her hand
In the cool silence of the room.

Flats in town, studios,
The gite in France
Surrounded by sunlight:
None could touch the
Magic of Sussex.
For this, he complied.

Her special house, full of friends
And family and music.
And wave on wave of
Talk, talk, talk
And radical thought.
And work, work. Always work.

High on the Downs two beacons stand
Broadcasting news, day and night.

She, the linchpin, followed him slavishly,
Created cocoons for him
Spun out of love. Year on year
Magicked a life for him:
Her trailblazing warlord,
High on his pedestal, worshipped, adored.

Under the Downs
Where two beacons stand

In silence he lies, sleeping beside her.
She whispers hauntingly, hold my hand.
Their hands which had fashioned much
Are now as still as a Knight and his Lady.
Here they will stay, immobile, forever:
Without colour. Without light. Without air.

She cannot reach him now.
– It was always so.

Sleepless Night

Can't sleep. I
Joffle and shuffle and
Wiggle and jiffle and
Shoffle and squiggle and squirm. I
Toss and I turn and I
Reel and I worm and I
Throw back the covers and then I
Lay on my side and I
Throw my arms wide and I
Pull back the covers and then I
Sigh and I yawn and I
Long for the dawn and I
Vacantly stare into space and I
Flop on my back then I
Itch so I scratch – here there and everywhere.
I'm so tired I'm so hot
I'm so cross that I'm not
Getting off to sleep.

If I get up
Would it help at all?

Down the stairs I could creep
And in the fridge peep
And snaffle a yoghurt or two.
Shall I make myself tea
Have it sugar-free
Count flies while I watch it brew?

What else could I eat?
Some cheese cut up neat
On a lump of granary bread.
I'd like a big slice
And biscuits are nice
But they always make crumbs in bed.

I think I'll stay put
Not asleep yet but
Maybe some Zen thoughts would do it.
Or maybe a prayer
If anyone's there.
Sing a pop song - that ought to do it.

I know what I'll do
Write a poem or two
Or a zealous counting of sheep.
Whatever it is
I must do it soon
For I'm nodding off to sleep!

Amazing

The air, the world, the night
Feel vast
And full of magic.
Across the fields an owl's hoot booms
As breeze-blown leaves crash overhead.
The river's ripple in a roar
And stars are fireworks, blazing.

But the searchlight moon cannot
Eclipse the light in your eyes,
Or the joy in my startled
Heart, at seeing you again.

Blue Stars

With you there would always be sunshine
In a small white house,
With its sunbleached furniture,
Waiting, in blue and white cool rooms.

On the tiny patio, beneath a quilt of indigo leaves,
A necklace of candles would shimmer.
We would sit side by side in silence,
Listening to the dark.

Your eyes are made for searching skies,
For scanning clouds' shapes and colours.
Moonlight would be soft and peaceful:
A time to share blue stars.

On the Edge

Long twisting lanes hurry to the sea
And rivers coil like grass snakes in the sun
Across sea-green fields stretched out,
Sunbathing, cooled by shady trees.

In hedgerows choirs of birds call and answer
And bluebell seas ripple deep in shadowy woods.
By roadsides, blankets of cowslip, campion,
Stitchwort, lie outspread on the grass.

The full stop of the Downs, above all.
Virginia's Downs, which constantly catch the eye,
The breath, the mind, with their beauty.
To the south, the sea gnaws their feet.

Why wasn't it here, on these dizzying heights,
Instead of in the flat lands below?
Here, where to look down on the sea,
Stops sight and thought and breath.

She chose the river, snaking in the valley,
To squeeze out her breath and thought and sight;
Hoping to be carried, stretched like a sunbather,
Bumping flowery banks, to the dual-faced sea.

Sketching Sissinghurst

Here in mauve shadows of autumn we sit
Drawing white beehives and grey apple trees,
In silence so deep we feel the earth turn.
Lights in the cottage are growing bright gold,
As our colours fade with each pencil stroke
And each minute slips away from our grasp.

At intervals acorns bombard the moat,
Their shock waves grey-muffled in ghostly mist
That weaves its dark way through trunks of gnarled trees,
Where blackbirds bustle and rustle red leaves.
Inside the cottage a silhouette moves:
The gardener, a giant from the past, glides by.

Her spirit wraps round us and weaves its spell
Drawing us in as night tightens its grasp.
She drifts through the orchard, turning the leaves,
Looks at the moon and a new-risen star.
Now hovers near to hear apples thud down
As, one by one, all are drawn back to earth.

Stopping on the Journey

On walks he always stopped
To look at other things:
Birds, trees, butterflies and the sky.
He pottered round his garden
Studying flowers, insects, growth and decay
And never failed to look up at
The moon and stars at night.
He lingered to look at sunsets,
Hills and valleys, blue-grey in the mist.
The scent of every flower he adored
And polish, cut grass, freshly laundered sheets.
He much preferred to stay and chat awhile to
Anyone, especially those he loved.
His journey was a joyful thing with many
Halts along the way. He enjoyed it all:
Far more than his destination.

Ancient Valentines

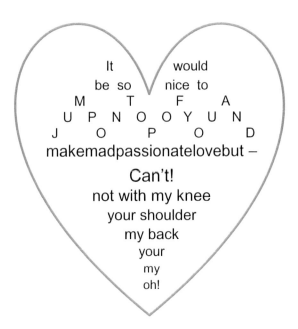

It would
be so nice to
M T F A
U P N O O Y U N
J O P O D
makemadpassionatelovebut –

Can't!
not with my knee
your shoulder
my back
your
my
oh!

Your Clothes

I love your clothes.
Your own scent lingers deliciously on them.
They were your choice
And now
They are part of you.

You wear them in that certain way
That I like.
They make you look even lovelier,
But
Like a present
I can't wait,
With trembling fingers,
To
Unwrap you.

In Bed

Listen to the rain, I say,
Then we close and kiss
We don't want to miss
A second of such bliss.

Hold me in your arms, I say,
Hold me, keep me warm
Save me from earth's storms
So safely here from harm.

Let us always stay, I say,
Close as this always
Tight-bound from the gaze
Of cold earth's staring ways.

Listen to the rain, I say,
There's no better sound
On earth to be found
When we're so closely bound.

Cross Words

In forty years, never a cross word
Until we started the daily

```
                        c

                        r

        w   o   r   d

                        s

                        s
```

Now we
```
            c                   s
                            d
                r       r

                    o

            w       s

        s                   s
```
                                    Daily!

Ancient Rebels

We haven't the time to polish up taps,
We're too busy now taking tea and naps
And wrapping up warm against the cold,
For that's what happens as you grow old.

Our hair has turned white and our knock-knees creak
We can't run fast though our bladders are weak.
We've flabby bits too awful to mention
But we don't care: we've got our pension.

Once we were timorous, now we are bold
We love being bossy now that we're old.
We've learnt to be wise, we've learnt to be patient,
It's all that's left when you are ancient.

The future hangs there like an albatross
It's frailty, sickness, memory loss.
But we'll Protest, Sit In, Know Our Rights –
Then have tea and toast and an early night!

Yes, we baby boomers will have our say,
And we'll never give up – not us. No way.
Our answer for those who call us "dear":
We may be ancient, but we're Still Here!

Garden in Summer

The marguerites fizzed
And the cow parsley frothed
And the columbines nodded and whirled.
The striped grasses reeled
And the astilbes smoked
And the lilies white pennants unfurled.

The roses stood straight
And bowed stiffly, a bit,
While the rock roses bubbled right over.
The small daisies jumped
Up and down with delight
And trampled all over the clover.

The peonies elbowed
Their way to the front –
They always expect the best view.
Such life and vitality
Here all around,
It makes me feel summery too!

Lizzie

Sunshine girl
Girl of golden laughter
And merry dancing sunbeam eyes.

Radiant girl
Radiating joy and life
And sunny welcome warmth and love.

Golden girl
Girl of sparkle, glitter
And dazzling day-long smile and fun.

Writer's Unblock
For Liz

Write anything, they said.
Write it down
It will work
It will return.

So he sat down and thought.
Thought about his afternoon:
Walking in sunshine
Admiring trees – some in bud –
And swathes of flowers,
Winding like yellow scarves
Under trees and over hills.
Then he stopped

And thought about
How much he had enjoyed it,
Until he had seen the steps again.
There, caught by her memory,
He had stopped.

It worked.
It all returned.
And he cried.

Winter in the Church

For George

Today there is silence, except for the clock
That ticks on loudly across the grey.
Today there is no-one but those entombed:
Feeling like them, she would gladly stay.

She sits in the pew that they sat in then
And still she feels he is sitting there.
They were part of the congregation once;
Part of the carols that filled the air.

But now at her side there is emptiness:
His St George hassock, discarded, lies.
And she who was happy that Christmas Day
Sits in the gloom, sees it all and sighs.

Lighthouse

Sailing single-handedly through the storm
I saw you wink your eye.
I steered for safety.

The wind roared in my ears
And the rain blinded me.
I almost capsized several times.
But I looked again for your light
And saw it trembling, gleaming in
The darkness, guiding me to safety.

I kept my sights on that intermittent beam
Fearful that I might lose it,
Fearful that when it went it wouldn't reappear –
But it always did.

Nothing could shake the lighthouse,
Not even the wildest of storms,
Standing firmly on the rocks
Foundations deeply embedded.
Overlooking all things,
Overseeing all things,
With its all-seeing constant eye, an
Unshakeable beam of light.

Thankfully I reached the harbour
And collapsed, exhausted, on the shore.
I never wanted to sail again.

I sold my boat.

I owe my life to the lighthouse.
How I admire it.

You're

You're an opiate with quicksilver laughter
An amalgam that can scatter like marbles
As enduring as granite
As mobile as magic.

You're as upright as an exclamation mark:
With ups and downs, a weathervane
Couldn't vacillate more, see-sawing
At the click of a kaleidoscope.

You're as introverted as a ball or
As expansive as spilt milk.
A fish isn't as elusive as you, or as shiny.
As wing-footed as sunlight

You're the hottest thing next to the sun.
You're a non-stop news bringer, that can flip
As silent and reflective as a mirror,
Dazzling someone close to you.

What's Not to Love?

You're my friend and you're my lover.
You're my mentor like no other.
All your qualities are hidden,
Loving father of our children:
For you're gentle, quiet and modest;
But of all men, are the strongest.
Always generous and patient:
And you're sexy though you're ancient!
And you have a sense of humour,
So I've heard - surely a rumour!?
Most of all I love your mind:
It's so clever, wise and kind.
You're the stars, the moon, the sea -
All things loved the most by me.

Of *'To Tish With Love'*, Janet's first book, (in aid of the Great Ormond Street Children's Charity) the stage, screen and TV star **Nigel Havers** said:

"A more delightful and heartfelt tribute cannot be imagined. I read each poem with a growing mixture of pleasure and sadness and congratulate Janet Beardsall for touching the heart in such a simple and tender fashion."

And of *'To Mum With Love'*, her second book (in aid of Hospiscare), the gardening writer and broadcaster **Anne Swithinbank** said:

"There's fresh emotion on every turn of the page as Janet Beardsall delights us with her poetry. Some funny, others sad and a few touching the core of human frailty, these lyrical verses will strike a chord with mothers everywhere."